What to Expect When You're **Busted**

Successfully Navigating the Maze of Probation and House Arrest

By
R. Scott Sandmeyer

Table of Contents

Introduction

Welcome to the crazy and difficult to navigate world of beginner's criminal justice! If this is your first contact with the system, either as a new arrestee or as the loving family member of one who is, this book is intended for you.

This is going to be a tough journey for you but it can be one that, with the right information, and sound thinking by you and the people around you, can be life changing for the better. This could be the journey that ends with you never landing in the criminal justice system again.

Getting arrested may be the harshest thing you or the person you're buying this for will ever face. If it is the last time because of something you have read here, perhaps the pittance you spent will have been worth it in the long run.

This is a no holds barred, real look at what it is like to be arrested, and face choices in and out of jail. Choices that may or may not be best for you or the one you're reading this for when it comes time to decide on a trial or a plea deal. Mistakes can have terrible consequences.

For 29 years I have worked in the criminal justice profession, and while I would like to think I have seen just about everything, I'm not that foolish. I am constantly amazed by the daily parade of insanities that come to my notice every day for the first time.

Before this, I was an officer in the US Navy. For several years I stood before the mast, as a division officer, with errant sailors for a variety of offenses against the Uniform Code of Military Justice.

In the service, the characters are essentially the same: Drunks, and drug dealers, spouse beaters, traffickers in stolen goods, thieves, fences, and others who for the first time, or repeatedly, made poor choices that landed them in trouble with the law.

More than anything, I want this to be a book filled with hope for you. I hope that you will be guided to make wise choices that lead to success while you are being supervised, and maintain this success for the rest of your life afterward.

This book anticipates many of the challenges ahead, including some "worst case" scenarios. It is designed to give you practical guidance to avoid things and situations that may prove harmful to you in the long run.
Finally, it should give you a firm foundation that results in never returning to the criminal justice system ever. Unless, of course, you would like to volunteer to help someone later!

Rest assured, though, that you can achieve longstanding success while you're being supervised and long after this brief period of time is over. In my time in this profession, I've seen the tide turned from where the majority failed in their first attempts to successfully complete their periods of supervision. Now, the majority succeed with the proper guidance and support of those who care about them.

Good luck in what you're dealing with and God bless you! If you're reading this for someone you care for, may your blessings and wisdom be multiplied. You'll need all of these things you can get.

R. Scott Sandmeyer
2016

Chapter 1 – Busted!

Alrighty then, let's begin!

Through whatever series of choices you or your loved one has made, suddenly the scene breaks to the back of a squad car on the way to your local jail.

A series of unfortunate events has led to one or more criminal charges against you and you find yourself in the uncomfortable position of being under arrest. The arrestee might find this emotionally and physically challenging for a while.

The physical discomfort may well depend on how much resistance was put up or how fast the person ran from the scene of the offense. From here on we will address the experience in the first person for ease of reference.

You will want this time to end as soon as possible because jail is a messy, dramatically ugly place to be and it is designed to be that way. It is hot in hot weather and cold in cold weather.

Squad cars and handcuffs are also not made for comfort either, although arresting officers are trained to make them as accommodating for you as possible. The more cooperative you are, the better.

Sometimes when someone is arrested, they resist so much that the police find it necessary to use pepper spray around the face and nostrils. If this happens, you will be suffering from lack of breath and sinus drainage like you have never experienced. Eye pain, too. You will require a long period of flushing out with cool water to get this stuff off of you. All while handcuffed.

In the probation office, where I supervise, I do not allow any staff member to handcuff anyone in front of their person under any circumstance and most police officers do not, as a rule, do so either. This is done for everyone's safety during the process and while you are being transported.

Depending on the jurisdiction, jail may not even be your next stop. Some cities have holding cells or vans where you may be held for an extended period until it is full enough to justify the expense of transporting enough people to the jail, which may be some distance away.

You may or may not be, at this point, handcuffed in front. If you are, it will likely be in shackles attached to your feet and you will be sitting on hard plastic or heavy gauged steel. These materials are used for ease of cleaning in case someone vomits, defecates or urinates inside the area in which you are sitting.

Once at the jail, there will be a booking process, including fingerprinting, perhaps DNA swabs, and breathalyzer testing. The usual things one sees on the Discovery Channel and

COPS. I'm taking it on a little faith here that almost everyone has seen a cop or jail show on TV, so bear with me.

Usually, within the next 24 hours, you'll be taken in your orange jail uniform and sandals, the usual jail attire in my jurisdiction, to what is called first appearance court.

PAY CLOSE ATTENTION HERE! Depending on what you do at this point, could make all the difference between having a permanent criminal record (if you have never had an arrest) and starting a series of errors based on misunderstood information. There is very little hand-holding in this process.

When you get the chance to make that first phone call, make it a good one. You'll need help from a criminal defense attorney if you can afford one. And someone to post bail so you don't spend unnecessary time in custody. As I said before, for the first timers, jail is a seriously uncomfortable place used to keep control of people.

If you can't afford a lawyer, well, like the cop told you, "one will be appointed for you". A bond will be set or, if you are lucky and the offense isn't serious and your criminal history is minor (perhaps a first offense) you may get released on your own recognizance with just a court date.

This is key: Under whatever status you are released, plan to be in court or be arrested. The judge will set a date and time right there in front of you when bail is set. You are responsible for that date and time.

Crimes come in two varieties, felonies and misdemeanors. Misdemeanors are considered minor, but can be punished by up to a year in the county jail in Florida. In some other states, misdemeanors can be punished differently.

Some misdemeanors can be violent and have an impact on how you might be supervised if you ever get arrested for a felony later.

You may be asked to enter a plea at that time. There is some potential for disaster here, too, if you are not thinking straight. It is not always best to take a deal on the spot, even if you will, as is so often said at this first hearing, "get out today". These are the options that will likely be placed before you:

- **Not Guilty** - usually guarantees setting bail and a future court date
- **Guilty** - does not guarantee sentencing at that time, depending on the crime
- **No Contest** - a lot like Guilty. Not admitting guilt but allowing what facts exist speak for themselves without making a defense

Often there is more than one offense and there is a bond imposed for each individual crime. You or your loved one will need to post at least 10% up front for each count you are charged with. In the county where I practice, each felony count starts at $5,013.

In addition to your possible release, you may be meeting with someone from my agency for what is called a Pre-Sentence Investigation. We'll talk more about these in the next chapter.

If you are released on your own recognizance, you'll be required to check in with a Sheriff's Detective at least weekly or more often. You may even be connected to an electronic monitor, depending on the risk of flight they think you present.

Since you will be in the community, you must stay away from people, places and things that will put you back in trouble again.

You have to have wise people around you who will help you. Also, you must hold yourself accountable. It all starts with you and it can be done. But don't take what just happened to you lightly. You must see this as the most important thing in your life.

Once you start on this road, there is no going back.

Chapter 2 – First Contact with Probation Officers

If your crimes are very serious, you may be staying in jail a while before you enter a plea or are found guilty by a judge or jury. That's where you will likely have your first meeting with a Probation Officer, commonly known as "the P.O.". This person may or may not be the one who supervises you if you end up on some community-based supervision program.

Once in a while, usually for first offenses that are serious, the judge will order what is called a Pre-Sentence Investigation, or P.S.I., for short. In Florida, these reports are done by the officers of my agency, the Florida Department of Corrections.

If you are a minor, a similar report called a Pre-Disposition Report, or P.D.R. is done, in the event the court wishes to place you in the Juvenile system.

Starting with this first meeting, it is important to understand something: The key to a successful relationship is to be as cooperative as possible. Honesty is the best policy. All of the information you give us will be checked and cross-referenced.

About this time you might be asking, "What would my Mom or Grandma say when that officer asks her that same question she asked me?" Lying always gets noticed and always gets mentioned in the recommendation to the court. Count on it.

We will be speaking to victims directly and having detailed conversations about the impact your crime has had on their lives, financial, emotional, and otherwise. Do not make the mistake of reaching out in any way to victims on your own or through a third party. People have a funny idea about what "third party contact" is these days, too. This includes:

- Sending flowers
- Twitter
- Facebook
- Letters
- Sending a mutual friend

By you or anyone else doing this on your behalf, a new crime may be charged. You definitely don't want that to happen.

Whether you are meeting the Probation Officer to be interviewed for a P.S.I. or for any other reason after you have been sentenced, cooperation and honesty are always expected. This is, after all, a business relationship.

Here are some of the ways uncooperative behaviors have manifested themselves in my experience with people being investigated or supervised:

- Outright lying

- Outright lying by those we contact to verify what you told us
- Making yourself unavailable for interview
- Being hidden by loved ones or friends
- Taking off before sentencing
- Victim blaming
- Hiding finances (especially if the crime is financial)

The list of ways in which the guilty, and you will be seen as guilty if you do any of these, is endless to those creative enough, devious enough, or desperate enough to try.

The funny thing is you're reading this here. If we have seen this, we have certainly thought of it. If you have thought of it, perhaps your creativity is best focused on ways of putting this behind you.

Chapter 3 – Sentencing

Now we get to sentencing. This is the "moment of truth", as they say. Whether you have endured the long, arduous process of a presentence investigation or have just decided to cut your losses and take a plea to end your time in jail, this will be the day the judge finally decides what to do with you.

Pre-Trial Intervention (P.T.I.) is a possibility that might be available to you if you are aware that it exists. Sometimes, in a rush to get to sentencing and get out of jail, this gets passed over but it may be a huge opportunity to get this first felony sealed, or even expunged.

P.T.I. is handled by the State Attorney in Florida and is a contract that you sign. It is similar to probation but is all done by letters between you, the State's Attorney, and the Defense Attorney.

After you have complied with all the terms, a letter gets sent to the State and hearing is set before a judge and then you're off. This keeps almost everything out of the court, a jury, and shortens the time you'll be supervised, as a rule.

But, for now, back to the podium, and sentencing.

Probation, Community Control, Electronically-monitored Community Control, Split Sentences, and the list of possible sanctions go on and on. If you don't know what to do, consider the following:

If you have a Public Defender (PD) God Bless you! That poor soul is several times more overburdened than the probation officer whom you may get to supervise you if you decide to take that deal that "gets you out today". They usually have many dozens of other people just like you that they are representing, so don't count on getting a whole lot of time and attention.

In my jurisdiction, there are just enough PDs to handle one meeting with you before you enter a plea and get sentenced the same day. Often, they will give a cursory scan of your file before telling you to cut your losses while they hold your hand in court.

Sorry, that's what happens most of the time with a PD unless we're talking about a major crime. Then you might have more than one conversation.

You get to the podium where you'll be met by another person in a suit: An Assistant State's Attorney. Police Officers, Deputy Sheriffs, and Probation Officers tend to be on their side in most matters, in case you were wondering how lopsided things can get.

The lady or gentleman in uniform standing tall and nearby behind you with a forearm on the Taser and the other on a sidearm will be a bailiff, just in case you get out of hand or need to go someplace you'd rather not go after hearing what the judge decides.

Well, this leaves the Judge in your case. You remember – the one who ordered the PSI and PDR in the last chapter.

By this time the investigating officers have talked to everyone, including the police, the State Attorney, and your Defense Attorney, not to mention the victim. You should have been praying that everything lined up your way and everyone in your corner was cooperative. You especially.

Judges know that a certain amount of gamesmanship goes into the statements made by those in your corner and those who would like to see you, please forgive the Pulp Fiction movie reference, have an "Ezekiel 25:17" experience.

Times have changed often in the 29 years I've been doing this and the mood of the public concerning crime and punishment, along with the attitudes of elected officials have a lot to do with how people are sentenced.

In Florida, where I practice, they have even changed the name of the code used for sentencing, without really changing how scores are applied. It used to be The Florida Sentencing Guidelines. Now, it is called the Florida Criminal Punishment Code.

The point of this is that, like a Sword of Damocles or a pendulum blade over your gut, sentences swing according to mood, just as much as anything else guided by politics. One thing you NEVER want to do is waste the court's time, or a jury's, with an unnecessary trial, if the facts point heavily against you. Any lawyer will tell you that.

I'm not a lawyer, but time is something no court has and to waste it is worse than the crime you may be accused of. You may even be guaranteeing a worse punishment for pleading not guilty.

OK, here we go. You're up there. Your lawyer is up there. The prosecutor is up there. And one, or maybe two, bailiffs in uniform are standing nearby.

Your brain is in turmoil. Maybe you're panicking about what will come out of the judge's mouth next.

Breathe slowly through your nose and do your best to be calm and hear what's being said. Try to take out the emotions of this terribly tense moment in your life. If you have family there, they're feeling at least as much tension as you are probably, so you need to be calm for their sake.

Families want to support their loved ones, and who can blame them? I have heard several schools of thought about having too many family members in court, but children present unique issues. You just never know how the court might look at your situation with them there. Will the judge be harsher or will the judge go easier?

Judges can do anything within the law based on what you have pled to or have been found guilty of. Crimes are felonies or misdemeanors and both can land you in jail. If you are on probation, this is a horse of a different color which we'll discuss later.

There are enhanced penalties depending on the harm you brought to each victim and the previous convictions you've had. If you are already being supervised, you can be hit for that, too.

Felonies are categorized this way. In Florida, the Criminal Punishment Code has a lot to do with what I'm about to tell you below so think!

- Third degree – punishable by up to 5 years in prison. This is the starting point every good prosecutor will come at you with to scare you. Trust me, you will be and should be. If you were foolish enough to put yourself in the situation that landed you here, your mind is in a head-spin about now.

  If this is the first felony and there is no violence or injury involved, you may not be looking at any time beyond what you have already done, but this is by no means certain.

- Second degree - punishable by up to 15 years in prison. In Florida, you are probably looking at some time up the road and then some time on community supervision after that, to make sure you don't fall back in the system again.

  - Most sexual offenses in Florida fall in this category, as well as DUI Manslaughter, Burglary of Occupied Dwellings, etc.
  - I only cite the above offenses because they are so common in my state and because I have seen so many people go to prison for them, but this list is by no means exhaustive as you can tell.

- First Degree and First Degree Punishable by Life (PBL) - The most serious of offenses for which prison sentences up to and including life imprisonment can and have been handed down include various forms of Drug Trafficking, Capital Sexual Battery (these would be victims 12 or under), Armed Robbery with a Firearm and various other crimes of violence including Homicide.

  - Don't make the mistake of believing you can't get a life sentence in Florida if you haven't killed someone.
  - These sentences are not normally accompanied by any community supervision afterward.

The possibilities for what a judge can do with you are endless depending on the crime you've been convicted of or copped to and many judges can be very creative in their sentencing practices.

In Florida we use what are called graduated sanctions, We've already talked about Pre-Trial Intervention, so I won't go into that here. This would be the best thing you could get, though.

Graduated sanctions are sort of like running bases in a baseball game, but each base is a violation of supervision. Think of home plate as the ultimate disaster. That's right – state prison.

Pay attention: This doesn't mean you might not go to jail or prison after hitting first base. Remember, judges are the final say at every point in the process.

The sanctions go like this:
- Pre-Trial Intervention
- Mainstream Probation (or just Probation)
- Drug Offender or Drug Court Probation
- Community Control (or House Arrest)
- Community Control II (Electronically Monitored)
- Sex Offender Probation (may include Electronic Monitoring)
- Sex Offender Community Control (House Arrest with Electronic Monitoring)
- State Prison

Depending on the crime, not all of these will apply. Not all offenses are related to drugs or sexual violence. As we will see in the example below, sometimes first offenses can be treated more harshly if the judge thinks that circumstances warrant it.

And away we go!

You've just been sentenced to Community Control for 2 years, followed by Probation for 4 years. You stole a loaf of bread and then ran "past all points of sale", as the arrest report said. To make matters worse, on your way out you ran into an elderly woman and took her purse, knocking her down to the ground.

Because of your age and the fact that you're a first offender, the judge sentenced you as a Youthful Offender. A youthful offender is sentenced as an adult, but the law can apply to anyone up to the age of 24.

Not every state has this. In Florida, this is good for any combination of sentences equaling six (6) years, including prison. I have seen first offenders accept prison sentences that result in "boot camp" which is a few months long and then get released to a community program lasting the rest of the period on probation.

This could have gone a whole lot worse for you, but not to worry – there's still time to snatch defeat from the jaws of victory with a few more poor choices.

By stealing the elderly woman's purse and knocking her down you committed a Strong Armed Robbery (good for 15 years) and Battery on an Elderly Person (If they chose to charge you), which is another 5-year felony.

Depending on how many store thefts you've committed, that may or may not be a felony. Three and up ices it as a felony in Florida.

You'll get out of jail today! Since you took the deal that got you out of jail today, you'll have to sign for it.

At the podium, the Judge will ask you if you made this decision of your own free will if you were pressured in any way, and if you are under the influence of any alcoholic or narcotic substances. You'll be replying "No, Your Honor" to all of these as you raise your handcuffed right hand swearing this is true. You may be handcuffed if you are being sentenced from jail. Otherwise, you will be free to raise your hand unshackled...this time. In some cases, they uncuff you before you reach the podium.

If you were in jail, they don't just uncuff you and trust you to bring back the jail's orange, blue, pink, white or striped scrubs and shower sandals. You'll be going back to jail for out-processing. This could take anywhere from 2 to 4 hours or longer.

If you're one of the many hundreds who will be electronically monitored, someone needs to come to the jail with specific training and expertise to get you connected to the equipment that will track your every movement.

Before you leave the courtroom you'll be fingerprinted and given directions where to go to the probation office for instructions and another set of directions after that.

From this point on, accountability sits squarely on your shoulders. Make no mistake about this. Smiling attorneys, bailiffs, correctional officers back at the jail can do nothing to get you anywhere. You must rely on the directions you have received and act immediately!

We'll talk about what's next in Chapter 4. You're in for a few surprises.

Chapter 4 – Free at Last?

Alrighty then! You've just been sentenced and now the officer in court has given you directions on where you are to go next. You might be in a bit of shock and may not feel like it. You may even want to get out of the building as quickly as possible and forget what just happened.

DON'T! Failing to follow up now is the fastest way to re-arrest and jail that you will find, so follow directions to the letter! These reporting instructions are time sensitive and often non-negotiable.

They will be given to you, and scanned or faxed to the office where you'll be sent next, so they will be expecting you. Don't just throw them away. Follow-up and be responsible.

If you were being held in jail, you will be given a certain amount of time, but you will be no less accountable. Very few jurisdictions provide transportation for you to get around. You may get a bus pass that is good for a day, but that is no guarantee. You'll have to make the best of it.

Make sure you have a good set of connections for rides and a place to stay for at least the first 48 hours after you get out so that you can get to the probation office and get things underway with the least amount of hassle.

If you have been ordered to be electronically monitored, you won't be leaving either the jail or courthouse immediately. In my area, electronic monitoring is done by the state agency responsible for being the eyes and ears of the judge. That would a Probation Officer.

After all is said and done and you have gotten to the probation office, you'll be taking a seat in a large room or small room with lots of chairs and maybe lots of people.

If you have kids you're responsible for, try to leave them at home. Just like courthouses, we all want support but this is really no place for them.

If you think this sounds insulting, it's not meant to be. This comes from nearly 30 years of experience watching successive generations of people come through the doors of probation offices, children in tow, who then witness what is done to their parent or parents, and then finding it all part of the normal routine of life. Some common sense can go a long way and you can do something about it just by limiting what they see of your personal business.

While in the lobby, you may get the urge to go to the bathroom. You should try to resist this. Why? You guessed it-urine testing! Even if you just got out of court or jail the same day, some officers are just suspicious enough to think you want to get that "one last (your drug here) in thinking there would be no consequences.

Probation officers are people just like you and me. This is a business relationship.

Officers are not your friend, pastor, guru, imam, parent, guidance counselor, or therapist, regardless of how they come across to you.

They are officially sanctioned, occasionally armed, certified law enforcers who are the eyes and ears of the judges who put you where you are. You agreed to this deal. They are here to see to it that you live up to the bargain and assist you in getting to the end successfully.

Systems and supervisors are in place as safety nets to keep the system intact and protect you, the officer, and the public from mistakes - yours or anyone connected to you.

Public safety is the overriding concern at all times. This includes your safety, too. Sometimes our cases become victims.

Your arrest, with or without a warrant, is always on the table if someone's safety might be at risk. Think about this if you're a drug user and parent, by the way. You won't be told by us if you have a warrant, but you're welcome to ask anytime.

Speaking of warrants, several things might have happened by the time you shake hands with your new officer. I say "might" because sometimes not all of the information that was available at sentencing was sent and may still not be available when you meet.

Some of those sentenced are so efficient or fearful (and this isn't necessarily a bad thing, at first) they get to the office before word of their sentencing is even sent by email to the officer.

In any case, one of the first things officers will have done, or have done for them, is a computer check to see if you have a warrant for you that may have been missed in court or by the jail.

Hopefully, there is no warrant to be served, and business can proceed. Otherwise, you know what's coming.

One last thing. The definition of the word "immediately" can be critical to your success on day one of probation or whatever sanction you're facing.

If the officer at court or jail gave you instructions to report to the probation office IMMEDIATELY, this means exactly what it sounds like.

Merriam-Webster defines it this way: (1) with no person or thing in between; (2) without delay.

If this sounds like a test of character, in a way it is. It is a basic test of your ability, and desire to cooperate and keep your end of the agreement – the contract - you've just made with your judge.

It happens occasionally that we seek warrants for people who have agreed to the terms of supervision, only to never follow-up by doing this first simple thing, IMMEDIATELY. If you can't or don't want to, don't make the deal. If things are getting in the way, call the officer or the officer's supervisor right away.

Back to the lobby.

First, a well-organized Community Control (CC) Officer will be coming to get you in the lobby. Don't be freaked out when the officer insists on walking at least arm's length behind you down the hall to their office. Security and safety are expected and we don't know you.

From here, you may expect about one hour of briefing and signing documents that will be the foundation of your freedom from now on. Pay close attention and ask questions.

Attitude is everything so be polite when asking. Leave any bad attitude you may have outside the building before you come in. A sense of offense breeds offensive words and behavior. It's your choice.

It doesn't always happen in the same order, and you may even have the same thing happen more than once in different locations. It just depends. We're pretty uptight about covering all the bases where I work.

You may get fingerprinted in the courtroom and get a DNA sample collected at the courthouse, even if you had this done at jail. You may have this done again at our office, simply if we can't confirm that it was done at the courthouse or jail.

Likewise, if we can't confirm that your digital photograph was taken there, we'll be doing that, also.

WAIT! DIGITAL PHOTOGRAPH?!? That's right your picture on the Internet. Along with your record, your address, and how much time you'll be supervised for. Only with very rare exceptions, like Pre-Trial Intervention, is this not the case.

Here's a brief list of the most important forms you'll have explained to you, and that you'll sign for on day 1. In no particular order:

- Generic Orders of Probation or Community Control - more on this later; this is not the official or certified copy signed by the judge, most likely. It's a summary of the general rules you'll be living by for the near future.
- Instructions to the Offender - depending on the state you're sentenced in, this is called by various names but the idea is to give you some helpful information to deal with your new life under supervision. Grievances, emergencies, restoration of civil rights, and so forth.
- The rest depends on the state, and may not even be done. In Florida, where I serve, I see cases that come

in from other states some of which have these, some that don't. If you come to Florida, they apply regardless:

- ○ H.I.P.A.A. - Healthcare Insurance Portability & Accountability Act form
- ○ Release of Information - for evaluation findings to come to the officer

The rules of pretrial intervention, probation, even community control are fairly basic. Community Control, as you will see later, has a lot more scrutiny added to it. Electronic Monitoring has even more than that.

Here are the basic rules of probation:

- Report once a month, or when you are told
- Pay costs of supervision
- Don't change your residence or job without permission first
- Don't violate any law and report every contact with law enforcement
- Don't associate with anyone engaged in any criminal activity
- Don't possess any firearms, ammunition or weapons
    - ○ Possession means what it sounds like: have in your hands
    - ○ Some orders say "own" also. If you are ordered to sell it, someone has to do it for you so you won't possess it

- o If the crime involved a firearm, you'll sometimes be ordered to forfeit it
- Don't consume alcohol to excess. Nor any controlled substance, unless prescribed by a physician
- Submit to substance abuse testing
- You will make a full and truthful report to your officer

This is what you can expect after you have completed some or all of the two years community control the court placed you on at sentencing. The next chapter lays out what you are responsible for while under house arrest. These conditions are even more rigorous.

Chapter 5 – Community Control

The case of the youngster in our scenario is not unusual. More often, though, a community control sentence comes as a result of a violation of probation. You might recall the graduated sanctions we discussed in the chapter on sentencing.

But let's not talk about failure right away! Remember that attitude is everything. Life is 10% what happens to you and 90% what you make of what happens to you. So let's assume you'll be successful and that you have started off on the right foot.

The good news is these caseloads tend to be rather small because people are getting more and more successful in leaving the system quickly.

First, Community Control doesn't tell the whole story. The community isn't controlling anything here. All of this relies on your personal control and your ability to stick to a rigid, barely negotiable schedule that you and your Community Control Officer plan on, and agree to, in advance.

You are permitted, in Florida, 30 minutes travel time to and from any point of travel to get where you're going and that's it. Less time, depending on where you need to go. Nearly always, it depends on what you have agreed to with your officer.

An important principle for you to master in your mind is this: House Arrest instead of Community Control.

You need to stop thinking of your CC Officer as your officer and start thinking of her or him as your jailer or warden.

"Why?" you might ask. The answer is very simple - House Arrest means that except for approved activities on the schedule you're about to complete, your home has now become your cell. These go along with the earlier rules of probation from the last chapter.

We're not just going to let you write down what you want to do on a schedule, and then let you go, just because it is in writing. Your officer has to be accountable for what he or she allows you to do, too.

In general, the guidelines are that you may leave your residence 30 minutes before going to any of these approved activities:

- Legal work, that has been verified by the officer
- Religious activities for a specific time, once per week
- Court-ordered activities
- Weekly reporting to the CC officer
- Grocery shopping and laundry, if someone else in the house can't do it

After the last activity of the day, you'll be granted 30 minutes to get home. Don't dilly-dally with stops of any kind.

The big thing to remember is **DON'T GAMBLE!** Don't gamble that you might be seen in a place you're not supposed to be and that isn't on your schedule. One of the reasons these caseloads are low is that officers are usually on the street checking where you are supposed to be, and occasionally arresting those who aren't. Chance meetings happen all the time. I'll leave the worst case scenario to your imagination.

House Arrest is very demanding but at least you don't have what's called Electronically Monitored Community Control. This is sometimes called Community Control II. That means all your movements are automatically tracked and recorded in real time. No matter what you tell us, your movements are known.

Since you are just on basic Community Control, we'll start by asking a lot of questions about your movements.

Do you or someone else do the laundry or grocery shopping? Do you have a washer and dryer inside of your home? If not, where do you do your laundry? If you do the shopping, where?

Make sure that you hold on to each and every receipt as verification. Do you know if we check where you say you went shopping? No! And we will not say.

Do we talk to employers? Absolutely! In Florida, only an order from the court will keep us from doing so. Be ready.

Oh, we may give you a little time to clear things up with your boss, but you'll need to make it quick. Officers have a limited amount of time before their file is reviewed and this will be one of the things that is checked.

My best suggestion is to be honest with your employer. Let them know you have made a mistake and are working hard to transform your life because of this. Don't make your future about this.

The burden of truthfulness rests squarely on your shoulders and you should take it most seriously.

You can generally count on a visit from one of my staff within 24 hours. We will do what is called a "walkthrough" of your place. Some places may even get searched if the court order calls for it.

Make no mistake, Community Control, and many initial probation visits for people that have never been through the experience might be a very invasive process. These "invasions" are legal, expected, and something you'll need to get used to.

Chapter 6 – Invasion

The walkthrough referred to earlier is short for "walk-through visual inspection". It's not a search but the officer, maybe with a partner, will be taking a look at where you live and who is in there with you. Some people may consider this an invasion, but it is part of what our job demands.

Inspections vary depending on who you are and what the charge is. What we check for may vary, too. This isn't an inclusive list, by any means:

- The common areas of the house
- Where you sleep at night
- The names and ages of others in the house
- Animals
- Who the owner is or who is on the lease

There are many things that distinguish this from an actual search and you will immediately know the difference when it happens.

When a search is ordered, here are some other things you might expect:

First, when agents of my office conduct a search of your residence, we will not be doing so alone. We may or may not be coming with local police in a backup role.

Second, it will be unannounced and at an inopportune time.

Third, we'll come in large enough numbers to take control of you, and everyone in your residence immediately. It is possible that your neighbors will be aware of what's going on if your status wasn't known to them already.

We don't kick in doors. We will ask respectfully and let you know that we are there to conduct a search. You should let us in. Declining will be a violation.

When you let us in, everyone will be herded into one place and watched. You'll probably be handcuffed. If anyone is sleeping, they will likely be awakened so they can be watched and controlled, too. Sorry, but this is for our safety and for the preservation of anything that might be destroyed that they can put their hands on.

Neither you nor anyone else will be making phone calls during this time, either. Your home or the place where you are putting your head at night has just become ours.

The limits of our search area in a residence you do not own include the space you sleep in and all the common areas you share with anyone else. We probably determined this when we did the walkthrough.

Of all the times of your life, while you're being supervised, this may be the most stressful you'll experience, and for good reason.

No one likes to have anyone in their personal, private business, especially in front of family, friends, and possibly neighbors.

What are "common areas"? They are places like:

- The living room
- Kitchens and all cabinets
- Bathrooms in the main area
- Hallways and closets
- Attics
- Basements
- Garages
- Porches
- Yard areas
- Your bedroom and any dressers

We will be lifting up and looking under things, through things, and moving things. We'll be asking you questions about things in the process in case there is anything we think might need explaining.

All this and no warrant. You're reading this correctly. No warrant.

The reasons aren't complicated, either. Some of the other uncomplicated ways that judges express themselves on their orders (that you agree to) include, but are not limited to:

- Search and Seizure Without a Warrant

- Search and Seizure
- You Will Submit to a Search of Your Residence, Person, and Vehicle

And one you may not even be aware of,

- Standard Drug Conditions (SDC)

In Florida, Standard Drug Conditions include a search of your residence and seizure of any contraband.

Let's talk about contraband.

Generally speaking, contraband is anything you are prohibited from having by virtue of the conditions of Community Control and Probation you agreed to when you signed on the dotted line.

Even the word "contraband" can have a broad range of interpretation depending on your offense, your conditions of supervision, and who is in the residence with you, among other variables.

Remembering that you were convicted of the offense of Strong Armed Robbery, this really doesn't give us anything to isolate as far as a theft target. I mean, you stole an old lady's purse and some bread. We won't be looking for a large haul of rye, pumpernickel, and purses unless something strange came upon in your background check.

More likely we will be targeting something more specific you may have stated to us, or an arrest in your past, maybe as a juvenile, that is a problem or concern that could derail you in the long term if we don't address it now.

The contraband could be any variety of drugs, drug paraphernalia, child or adult pornography - if it is child porn, it is always illegal and you will be going to jail - if it is adult porn you don't have to worry because you're not a sex offender. More contraband could be any kind of firearm, ammunition, or other weaponry.

I won't be giving you much detail about how we go about this because an element of doubt, fear, and a pervasive sense that you won't know what's coming next works to our advantage.

If we find illegal drugs of any kind in an area controlled by you directly, with certainty you'll go to jail.

The same is true if we find firearms, ammunition, or anything that by you simply having it is illegal, you'll go to jail.

This may mean you have to know and trust the people you are living with.

If you are old enough you may have heard one or both of these: "Blood is thicker than water" and "honor among thieves". Don't you believe it.

I have seen the parents of people we supervise throw their adult children under the bus during a search when they didn't want to take the fall for *their* illegal activities in front of police who were assisting us.

Let's get things back to normal, so you can get on with your life. O.K.?

Chapter 7 – What Else?

Well, let's just hope that the aforementioned search didn't result in anything bad getting found, or your arrest, or your host asking you to leave after our intrusion into your and their life.

These things can and do happen and only serve to destabilize an already shaky situation. Maybe it won't happen to you. But like I said before, if your number comes up, it will happen.

Better to move along and stay focused on the things you have to get done to stay compliant.

Back to the business at hand.

In no particular order, community control and probation orders tend to follow the same format in nearly all 50 states, with some variations. In my state of Florida, the conditions and special conditions tend to be more rigorous. Not all states have community control.

Florida has 67 counties and the special conditions will vary depending on the county or judicial circuit in which you are sentenced.

"Special Conditions?" you might be asking. Yep. These are conditions designed for you to accomplish three things:

- First, address particular needs of yours so that you never come back into the criminal justice system again
- Second, to properly compensate your victim and make them as whole as possible for your crime, and
- Third, to compensate the community, because your offense is putting taxpayers and other law-abiding citizens out in some way.

First, let's get down to the basics for everyone. Standard Conditions of Supervision.

Because you are starting out on Community Control, the rules are quite a bit more rigorous than they are for others that would be on just Probation but, assuming the positive, your time could come even sooner and not because you did something wrong and found yourself in court facing revocation of that Community Control. Great job!

At the judge's discretion, and with your Officer's recommendation and no objections by anyone else, you could end your period of house arrest earlier. A lot has to go right for this to happen, but it does happen and we do recommend it from time to time.

No matter what, it is the judge's court and he or she can do as he or she pleases.

The main difference between Probation and Community Control has to do with when you are allowed out of the house, where you are allowed to be, and when you must report to your Officer. It really is about that simple. If you try to make it more complicated than that, you'll risk overthinking things and get yourself in trouble.

Remember what I said before: At this point in your supervision, your relationship with your officer is the same as the one you would have if you were an inmate in jail. That officer is your jailer. Anything you want to do requires permission first and your home is your cell.

While under house arrest you'll be reporting at least once per week to submit a proposed schedule with the necessary, and I mean necessary things you need to do to comply with your orders, live a law-abiding life, and stay home.

After your schedule is approved by your CC Officer, you'll get the original and we keep the copy. You'll bring that original back the next week so that we can compare what you submitted to us, with what we can prove you actually did during the week.

If you have violated house arrest, a warrant can be obtained quickly. Occasionally, with good reason, some are arrested without a warrant.

You can try to fudge by being out in the middle of the night or getting friends or family to lie for you, but their verbal report to us carries absolutely no weight. If our eyes are not on you personally when you are supposed to be home, or wherever you are supposed to be on that schedule, the jig is up!

We usually don't spill the beans to friends and family what the rules are. They are not the ones who are responsible for your signature. You are.

Don't ask me why, but the next standard condition is a financial one. Sometimes the court will waive it, but usually not. This is the Cost of Supervision. Usually, it is between $40 and $50 per month for each month you're being supervised. These are costs in addition to court costs, fines, restitution, drug testing fees, and any other fees associated with any other court-ordered thing you must accomplish.

If you are getting the idea that freedom is not free, you're on track. In fact, things associated with community supervision are a cottage industry in most states, particularly so in Florida, where I practice.

More on movements. Whether you are under house arrest or probation, you can't merely pick up and change residences or jobs without permission. And permission means just that. It is not making changes and then letting us know after the fact, although many think a cozy relationship earns this privilege.

You should never make any assumption like this, no matter how comfortable you feel the relationship with your officer is becoming.

As if the earlier search may not have convinced you, the next standard condition is to allow us to visit your residence and your job. Your job, if it is necessary and we can't obtain the information we need by a phone call. Even if we have all the information we need, we may need to see you on the job to see if you are telling us the truth about your movements.

This next standard condition is the cornerstone of all community supervision in every state, no matter how it's worded. It's a catch-all condition that, if you read it carefully and adhere to it, is designed to keep you out of situations that lead to any arrest for any reason. It's amazing how often this particular condition gets violated every day by people under supervision.

Specifically, the statute says "Live without violating any law. A conviction in a court of law is not necessary in order for such a violation to constitute a violation of probation, community control, or any other form of court-ordered supervision".

If you are ever lucky enough that you land on what's called Administrative Probation, this is the only condition there is. You pay a $50 administrative fee, we do a little paperwork and you hit the road. Hopefully, we never cross paths again and you never break the law again. This happens only on rare occasions though and it won't be happening in the case of our young man under house arrest.

Notice what I call the "catch-all" provision. That's the part that says "a conviction in a court of law is not necessary..." The mere fact that you get arrested is enough for us to have your supervision revoked and any prison time you might have gotten before, you may get now.

Sometimes, someone will get cited for an offense and not get arrested. This condition still applies. A citation is as good as an arrest. Often, people will come to the office with a traffic citation or some other citation for a criminal offense, and then minimize what they did.

They'll say something sheepish like, "I wasn't arrested, but the cops gave me this", or "my lawyer says this will get dismissed anyway".

These statements may be true to a point but they make you no less guilty of a violation. Often, we have been notified of your citation before you have had a chance to cook up an alibi for it anyway. Don't waste your time.

As a supervisor of officers, I am especially sensitive to this point and I can guarantee that my superiors are, too. If something big goes wrong with your case, it could be our backsides in the wringer with you. This is why a violation report will always be submitted to the court.

The next condition we'll talk about may be just as big an issue as the last one for some of you to keep, just because of the company you keep. Often, people doing the right thing will be thrown under the bus by people close to them doing the wrong thing.

Because you're the one being supervised, when police arrive anywhere, you're the one most likely with the biggest bull's eye on you.

Get it straight! Even if you're not the one driving that got pulled over while drunk, or the one carrying the drugs, if you are under house arrest or have a curfew and can't reasonably explain your presence in that situation, your life just got immeasurably more complex.

If the police can't raise someone from community corrections late at night, or the coin doesn't drop your way if they can, you may be going to jail that night. The police and that probation supervisor they called may both be wrong, but you'll spend time in jail waiting to find out. There is nothing you'll be able to accomplish or undo at this point.

The wording of the Florida condition goes like this: "You will not associate with anyone engaged in criminal activity." Other states have a similar condition with the similar intent that you stay away from people that will lead you astray.

Here's a thought: You are an adult. No one is going to hold the other guy accountable for leading you anywhere.

Most often, this condition will come into play just outside Florida's community corrections' drug labs. Every probation office has one.

Some courts go as far as naming individuals that you must stay away from. Not just the victims, but co-defendants in your offense. You may be a member of a gang or have a friend in a gang. You'll have to stay away from them, too.

We'll look at some other situations where other people can get you into a heap of trouble later on, but let's move on with some more conditions.

It should be common sense but often isn't, that having a gun in your possession or ammunition or drugs (legal or not) is going to set off all sorts of alarms with your officer that might result in your arrest.

Drug testing is something we do with every person we supervise, no questions asked. We don't let you leave our office until you have submitted a urine sample for us to test. If the sample is positive for any illegal drug, and you admit that you used it, great!

The main thing is your honesty is usually rewarded by you not being arrested that very minute. Yes, it is a violation that we will take up with the court but this is a good start. You'll be signing an admission statement to what you used and when. We'll complete a report to the court and let them know you were honest with us.

Sometimes, people can't bring themselves to this level of cooperation and honesty. They take off. Or they deny they used. If they take off, their arrest comes sooner or later. If they deny, we send their sample to a lab for testing.

If the lab confirms the positive result, a violation report is done alleging several things:

- Illegal drug use or use of a legal drug in an illegal way
- Lying to the officer
- Possible criminal association

It is always better to be honest. It saves you time, and it may not result in your arrest. We're not trying to trip you up. If you have a problem, we want you to get help for it and get out of the system.

Possessing firearms and ammunition should not ever happen and is indefensible if you live alone. If you live with someone and these things belong to them, they should be locked away where only they have access to them.

Talk to your officer about everything that may be a problem area for you. If you are having a problem understanding something, don't try to make it seem like you have things under control.

This is a business relationship designed to benefit you. Lying doesn't just mean giving false answers to our questions. Don't hide what is harming your chances of being successful.

This is your life and we have a vested professional interest, beyond the end of probation, in seeing you prosper.

Chapter 8 – You Are Not the Victim

From the point of your arrest to the booking, to interviews at the jail, to the searching of your home, to the searching of your person when you get cuffed for violating your supervision you are going to feel like you took the wrong deal at sentencing.

Without much doubt, you will feel like a victim. You mustn't. You aren't. Remember the facts that put you here in the first place: You went into a grocery store and stole a loaf of bread. Then you knocked down an old lady in the process of stealing her purse. The rest of the story is contained by what you took out of her purse.

Here's where the victimization really begins. In addition to the physical and emotional harm you caused to the old lady (maybe there were broken bones and other physical injuries that required hospitalization and other therapy), there were credit cards, an ID card and a wad of cash that she now claims you took.

Prove you didn't take any of these things, especially cash. Who is going to believe you at sentencing? Victims get all the benefits of the court's doubt, generally, when it comes to monetary and other damages.

If you made any kind of a getaway, whether on your own or with someone else's help, the police are going to want compensation for their time and trouble, too. The taxpayer will want them to be paid back. After all, the public pays for the police.

These costs, in Florida anyway, are called Investigative Costs. Sort of a form of restitution you pay for the number of man hours they put into catching you. The longer it takes, and the more manpower they use, the more it will cost you in the long run. Sometimes these costs can run higher than the actual restitution to the victims!

Let's take a quick look at what the immediate costs of your crime are so far (just where it concerns the cops and the lady at the store):

- One loaf of bread
- Paramedic service for the lady
- Possible trip to hospital and emergency treatment in the ER
- Therapies received while in the hospital
- Follow-up treatment following release from the hospital
- Costs for anything bought with her credit card or another bank card
- Any claimed cash she successfully argued you took
- Investigative costs for each officer by the hour
- Costs of transporting you to the jail, and other costs while in jail

One more thing: these costs can go up if the victim's condition gets worse or she dies. You could even face re-arrest and an upgrade of your original charge.

There is a bright side in all this. You might have someone to share the expense of the crime with! We in the criminal justice field call this person a Co-Defendant. You might have heard them also referred to as an Accomplice or Accessory.

Why is this good? Well, you and your supposed friend didn't plan well enough how you were going to get away with all this. Now you can at least plan how you will get on with the rest of your life and, perhaps with luck, avoid going to prison.

This is what we call Joint and Several Liability. This means that responsibility for the payment of all restitution to your victim is shared between you and your co-defendant, no matter who had greater responsibility for the crime.

Sometimes this is applied to Investigative Costs, as well, if the costs are very high. Like I said before, in certain crimes the costs of getting you arrested and charged are higher than the actual take in the crime itself.

Long story short: If your co-defendant gets put on community supervision with you, or any other sanction in the community he or she shares all the costs. If he or she doesn't pay, YOU PAY 100%.

It's not 50-50. Everyone pays until the entire amount is settled to the court's satisfaction. Count on the victim or the victim's representative having a say at every hearing.

At every appointment, you need to make it your business to ask what payments have been made by your co-defendant. Maybe you need to ask if they are still being supervised, or if they have been revoked and sent to jail or prison. If that is so, you are now the sole proprietor of "Pay My Victim, Inc.".

What the heck! You don't even need to ask your PO for some of this information. You can check most state's public websites to see what your co-defendant's status is on your own. But whether you check or not, if your partner in crime quits paying, it's all on you, yet again.

Since this is the first chat about money we're having, here's the actual process we follow in Florida where I work (ideally):

- Accounts established at first meeting-input into the database
- You sign the agreement, it's not an agreement to pay so much as your understanding that you owe the money
- Your PO will point out the monthly amount you pay starting next month
- You get the original and we keep our signed copy

If all goes well, the other PO is doing the same if you have a co-defendant and there will never be a problem. What could go wrong? Right?

No drama. Just make your payments. Whatever other problems you have, if you have a victim, it is all about them.

Remember one thing, though. No matter how long it takes the first time you're in the PO's office, you should make it your business to get everything you need to get your payments set up after the first meeting. If you don't, you will find yourself behind very quickly.

One of the things in Florida is that all payments have a priority established in advance by the computer and restitution is always the first thing to get paid unless the court says otherwise.

One other thing about this payment, or any other kind of payment, if you fall short one month, do everything you can to make up for it, or get ahead the next month. There is never any harm in paying ahead. There is always the chance that a violation can result if you repeatedly fall short each month.

The more you can stick to the basics each time you see your officer, the better off you will be.

Chapter 9 – Drama Anyone?

In the 80's, when I started my career, it was unusual for one generation after another to find themselves in the criminal justice system in any way.

By the mid-90's, I started supervising families with parents, and occasionally children under sanctions in the same household.

By the 2000's, I was a supervisor and was reviewing work from my staff where several generations had been supervised and/or in prison.

This isn't meant to be a guilt trip or a sermon on how to live your life but Proverbs 22:6 is a great teaching point here: "Train up a child in the way they should go, and even when they are old they will not turn from it."

We all have the same 24 hour days in which we handle our business. What we *decide* to do with that time is what shows the world whether we are wise or unwise.

A patient suffering a heart attack is in crisis. Most of us have seen what an EKG looks like when someone having one is hooked up to the electrodes. It spikes up and down erratically unless there is some kind of immediate intervention. Eventually, the heart stops, brain activity ends, and the patient dies.

End of story. Unfortunately, lives in crisis tend to go the same way. Serious intervention is needed to avoid major problems.

One of the reasons supervision orders have a condition that includes not associating with those engaged in criminal activity is to avoid drama like this. Some people just dwell on it every day, though.

A mutual goal of the officer and person being supervised is to remove obstacles to success. Sometimes obstacles include people when they seem to be throwing things off course.

Familiar people, places, things, and habits are what can trap you in the life you will live, unless you choose to do something differently. I speak from personal experience here.
There are ways to overcome these bad habits that have led you to this crisis in your life and it all starts with a one-word response to drama and people who want to create and keep the drama in your life.

The word: **NO!**

That's right: No. You don't need to be cold, or rude, uptight, or mean-spirited about it. You may not be able, or even willing, to change your surroundings and you can't change your family. You may even rely on them.

But this doesn't mean you take the geographic approach to problem-solving. After all, you still have yourself and your baggage to carry and there may be a lot of it. Right now, the wheels on your luggage have fallen off. Let's get them back on and get you on track!

People in the real world outside are no different. There are good and bad, well-intentioned or ill-intentioned in every walk of life. Some of them may be family and friends. If you look at people carefully, "you will know them by their fruits", as it says in Scripture.

People who use other people may try to convince you that it is a moral lapse for you to put your needs and priorities first. Maybe this is what landed you in this situation, to begin with. If it is, "NO!" is an effective word for you.

Keep in mind, though: It may mean the temporary or permanent loss of a friendship or significant family relationship, especially if you're not meeting a demand of theirs.

You may get threatened, sworn at, have false claims made about you, or even smeared on social media. I've seen all of these occur. They're evil, but don't let them stop you!

Drama comes into everyone's lives in many unexpected ways. The impact drama has on you depends on how well you have prepared for the other areas of your life that you can control.

This isn't a chapter about planning every little thing in your life. Some people do. Planning is a good thing for the most important things and you must do some of this, most of the time.

Most people want two things in their lives: Influence and control. If you don't want these things, thanks for buying my book. You can stop reading now.

Well, now. You're still here. Good!

Here's where you gain understanding about how to gain influence and control over your life without someone in a suit and tie, or a uniform, badge, and body armor telling you.

Up to this point, we've more than covered a number of ways you can give up influence and control, or have it taken from you. Day to day is a fight to get it and keep it.

Habits are everything in the lives of the influential. I'm not Bill Gates and you probably aren't either (if you are Bill Gates, may I have a grant?). People like him, have successful people around him helping. Mentors, advisors, schedulers, and other talented people who allow them to do what they do best to stay at the top of their field, whatever that field is.

Because of this, these influential people exercise control over the smaller things that avoid what we have already discussed: Crises-both the number of crises and the severity of them.

Their ability to control the small things helps them to plan for the larger, more important things that advance their influence and help them to grow as human beings.

Amazingly enough, when you start getting success in your life, and I'm putting this in terms of who you are on purpose, the old people that led you to the current crisis of being in the criminal justice system will probably not hold the same attraction for you that they did when you were out there violating the law and hurting people like our young thief under house arrest.

When you are planning and focused, wasting time is never an option. I'm not talking about rest for the body. Rest and sleep are a must. The body can't take a lot of work in the course of a day, and then follow it up with hours of TV, or Xbox, PS4, or other online gaming.

If the well planned day leads to influence and control, then crises, interruptions, and dramatic people are things that will conspire to throw you off your plan. You sure don't need to give up influence and control by wasting the time you have left by overdoing leisure time activities.

When it becomes a pattern, it becomes a problem. When it becomes a problem, it may be the sign of a crisis. Eventually, it will reflect in ways that cost you.

These behaviors are certain signs of lost influence and control:

- Being habitually late anywhere
- Not planning
- Not working a plan, if you have one
- Not being accountable
- Not having wise advisors
- Not listening to wise advice if you have sound advisors

If these are things you have never done or people you have never had to help you, you'll have some challenges ahead of you, but influence and control will win out over drama, ignorance, poor planning, and just miserable errors of thought every time if you choose to make correct choices now.

Chapter 10 – The Mindset Thing

As we finish what I truly hope will be a life-changing read for you or the loved one you are trying to help, it is of overriding importance that all of the people around you understand and work toward your main goal of life:

Transformation.

That's right. Even if you are the loved one trying to be helpful, you probably have to make some changes of your own that will put you in a position to help, changes that will get your loved one through this ordeal without ever returning to the system.

Without transformation, this will not likely take place in any long term way.

Thought processes, how you communicate with people, how you go about your daily routine all betray who you really are. We as probation officers are trained to pick up on these things, especially old-timers like me.

Talk about mindset, we used to have a short class in our training academy called "Games Offenders Play". I'll bet you can guess what this was about.

To some extent, your mindset put you where you are. Your mindset will permit you to have, or deny you, the one thing you should most want in life: Transformation.

Here are some absolutes you must get a hold of, and CONQUER, from here:

- Much of what you are ordered to do, you will have no say over
- You can conquer your desire to flee from this consequence
- Expanding influence means leadership over yourself and your habits
- Mastering these things will lead you to transformation and a new mindset

If you have children, or if children in your life are around you, say a niece or nephew, younger brother or sister, or some other child you feel any attachment to, they look to you for one of two reasons: (1) A shining example of what they would like to be or, (2) An object lesson of what to steadfastly avoid.

What "normal" are you creating for that child in your life that you take for granted?

That transformation you are bringing about because you haven't been paying attention may not be what you want after all. Do you see my point?

I respect people of every background and faith, and as a Christian, I am commanded to love everyone, including those who hate me. This includes you. This is why I am writing this.

Wisdom comes from every direction when you seek it out. So does transformation. Even a sudden crisis, like an arrest, the death of a close loved one, a divorce, or some other disaster seldom bring about major life change for people in a positive way.

In fits of ugliness, people will sometimes call others names. Maybe you have been called an "animal", or had your parental lineage questioned, or much worse. If this happened to you when you were young (maybe you still are) and it happened a lot (or maybe it still is) it left scars.

People who do the name calling are worse because they are emotional and act on these emotions. The drama kings and drama queens in your life may have done lots of name calling pointed at you. Maybe it was a parent or someone you looked up to. It was probably done to them, too. It was their normal.

This was a transformative time in your life, wasn't it? And not for the better.

Wisdom is not reserved for the educated, the wealthy, or the well positioned. Just because you are in the system right now does not put a barrier to you getting some, either.

Wisdom, Influence, and Control combine to create this Transformation. These things are expanding or contracting and you need to make all of these things grow.

If you don't, they will shrink and ultimately reduce to a pinpoint. Back to square one for you. The only thing constant is change.

Everything you have read in the earlier chapters should have given you a pretty good idea of some of the many thinking mistakes that have contributed to what could be a great opportunity, or another disaster, in your future.

People, places, and things have already been talked about but they are the most important things. You have probably heard one or both of these things: "If you do what you have always done, expect to get what you have always gotten", or "The definition of insanity is to do the same thing over and over again, and expect a different result".

Both of these things are true and you will have to change some of the people, places, and things in your life for the long term to achieve a positive transformation. Remember that other people in crisis love you just the way you are and will fight to keep you that way.

The devil is in the details. He always has been. Wisdom comes from every direction to those who seek it out.

Whether you are Christian, Jew, Muslim, Hindu, or any other belief system, one of the greatest writings of wisdom ever created was written about 3,000 years ago by a man named Solomon.

Proverbs in the Bible.

Well documented as one of the wisest men of his or any other time, Old Sol wrote this short book of wisdom so that people would not be led astray by their own ignorance or innocence, the evil of others, or their own.

The unbelievable thing about Solomon is that he became so successful that he quit following his own advice and the advice of his closest advisors! Ultimately his country collapsed and within a short time, his people were enslaved and taken away captive to other places.

By the way - knowledge is NOT power, APPLIED knowledge is power. If you want a take away from any proverb, this is it! Now use it.

When Solomon stopped applying the knowledge and wisdom he had, everything came crashing down around him. He stopped being faithful to his principles, his family, himself, and his God. He led millions into slavery when he did this.

You can change that today. Now. If a bird sees a trap being set, it knows to stay away. Animals don't plan. They do this instinctively. You can plan and act on better instincts.

You make the choice:

Influence and control or crisis and enslavement. A well-executed plan or the influence and control of others.

The robbery of your time and resources by those who will dispose of you at the first sign of trouble or true friendship and guidance of wise people of redeeming value, who will value you forever.

Or you can do nothing. But think it through, not making a choice IS a choice and crisis becomes yours by default.

Our world today wants you to live by your emotions and little else. Feelings are all that matter out there and most people make decisions this way.

Knowledge, on the other hand, and wisdom, when you use it, screams at you to ignore your past and dump the foolish, childish emotions that have led you by the nose to the brink of lifelong ruin.

The life in control, on track, influential, at peace, productive and secure can be yours with effort, guidance, and proper and dedicated inputs.

Acknowledgments

Proverbs 15:22 says that plans go wrong for lack of advice, but many counselors bring success. I would like to thank these learned and dear friends for their cheerful support during the process of writing this, my first book:

Paul Campbell, a retired colleague and for years a strong spiritual support for me and dear friend. His level of faith has carried me forward for a long time. Much of the negativity that made its way into the first draft, made its way out after long discussions that started with him.

Joshua and Rebekah Hollis are young and well-educated friends of my wife's and mine. They bring a fresh perspective to about everything we discuss and have seen many come to faith through The Word.

Sarah Powell, another well-educated friend and fellow Scripture teacher at my church, who expressed great enthusiasm for the project as soon as she heard I finished it.

Cathleen Gill, a fellow professional and friend whom I've known for many years and kept the factual basis of my writing intact, where it concerned the mechanics of our trade.

My mother-in-law, Janice Collum, my most enthusiastic editor. She had wanted me to leave many of the personal anecdotes I had put in the book in, but I decided to save them for other works more fitting for specific topics. We spent a lot of time on the phone discussing things like parenting and how they fit into the scenarios

I put in, but edited out later. Wait until you see some of the later works.

Finally, my beloved wife, Sandy, who has laid out the manuscript and handled much of the web page for when I get ready to roll this out at publication time. She truly is the genius behind much of what I do. Platitudes laid down here hardly begin to do her credit. I love her so.

About the Author

Scott Sandmeyer has been a criminal justice professional in Florida for 29 years, the last 15 as a leader of other professionals in the field of community corrections. He has audited domestic violence programs and supervised people on various parole, sex offender, drug offender, and house arrest programs.

He is happily married to his wife of over 26 years, Sandy, and they have a 22-year-old son, Tim. Scott and Sandy are closing in on their Doctorate in Sacred Studies and Theology and Tim is attaining mastery as a Certified Transit Technician. They are all Christians and attend church in their hometown of Clearwater, Florida.

www.ingramcontent.com/pod-product-compliance
Lightning Source LLC
Chambersburg PA
CBHW060409190526
45169CB00002B/828